COOKIES
AND BARS

COOKIES
AND BARS

40 APPETIZING RECIPES FOR MOUTH-WATERING TREATS

First published in 2009
Love Food ® is an imprint of Parragon Books Ltd

Parragon
Queen Street House
4 Queen Street
Bath BA1 1HE, UK

ISBN: 978-1-4075-6835-5

Printed in China

Design concept by Fiona Roberts
Produced by Ivy Contract
Front cover photography by Laurie Evans
Front cover home economy by Lorna Brash

Notes for the Reader

This book uses both metric and imperial measurements. Follow the same units of measurement throughout; do not mix metric and imperial. All spoon measurements are level: teaspoons are assumed to be 5 ml, and tablespoons are assumed to be 15 ml. Unless otherwise stated, milk is assumed to be full fat, eggs and individual vegetables are medium, and pepper is freshly ground black pepper.

The times given are an approximate guide only. Preparation times differ according to the techniques used by different people and the cooking times may also vary from those given. Optional ingredients, variations or serving suggestions have not been included in the calculations.

Recipes using raw or very lightly cooked eggs should be avoided by infants, the elderly, pregnant women, convalescents and anyone suffering from an illness. Pregnant and breastfeeding women are advised to avoid eating peanuts and peanut products. Sufferers from nut allergies should be aware that some of the ready-made ingredients used in the recipes in this book may contain nuts. Always check the packaging before use.

Picture acknowledgment

Ivy Contract would like to thank Paul Webster/Stone/Getty Images for permission to reproduce copyright material for the endpapers.

Introduction

There is nothing to match the inimitable flavour of a cookie that has been freshly baked that day. Baking biscuits in your own kitchen is immensely satisfying (in fact, some don't even require baking). In addition, they're easy to make and take very little time, so you can whisk up a batch of tasty treats in no time at all. You can even encourage the kids — major consumers of cookies and bars, after all — to help mix the dough and cut it out. This could be a constructive and fun rainy-day pastime.

The recipes in this book are divided into four chapters. The first three feature chocolate, fruit and nuts, while the fourth offers some more elegant biscuits for special occasions. Among all these cookies and bars you are sure to find at least one that is perfect for morning coffee, afternoon tea, school lunch boxes, filling the after-school gap or serving with ice-cream for dessert. From family favourites, such as brownies and flapjacks, to delicate morsels, such as florentines and amaretti, you will be spoilt for choice.

Perennially popular with adults and children alike, chocolate biscuits, brownies and bars are, arguably, everybody's favourite sweet treat. Certainly, chocoholics will not be disappointed by the fabulous collection of recipes in this chapter, which includes everything from what might be described as the best cookie in the world – Double Chocolate Chip Cookies – to mouth-watering Caramel Chocolate Shortbread.

Cooking with chocolate is not difficult but it does require a little care. To blend chocolate with other ingredients, it usually needs to be melted. The easiest way to do this is to break it into small pieces and place them in a heatproof bowl. Set the bowl over a pan of gently simmering, not boiling, water and heat until the chocolate has melted. Do not let the base of the bowl touch

CHOCOLATE HEAVEN

the surface of the water and make sure that, if you are stirring the chocolate or a mixture of chocolate and other ingredients, water does not splash into the bowl because it will make the chocolate grainy and spoil the texture of the biscuit or its chocolate topping. You can also melt chocolate in the microwave. Break it into pieces and arrange in a microwave dish. Check with the manufacturer's handbook for timings, bearing in mind that white chocolate should be melted on medium, while plain or milk chocolate can be melted on high. Remove the dish and stir frequently to check whether the chocolate has melted. Chocolate can be melted over direct heat in a saucepan if it is combined with one or more ingredients, such as butter and syrup.

MAKES 24

115 g/4 oz unsalted butter, softened,
 plus extra for greasing
55 g/2 oz golden granulated sugar
55 g/2 oz light muscovado sugar
1 egg, beaten
1/2 tsp vanilla essence

115 g/4 oz plain flour
2 tbsp cocoa powder
1/2 tsp bicarbonate of soda
115 g/4 oz milk chocolate chips
55 g/2 oz walnuts, roughly chopped

Double Chocolate Chip Cookies

The minimum cooking time will produce cookies that are soft and chewy in the middle. The longer cooking time will result in crisper cookies.

• Preheat the oven to 180°C/350°F/Gas Mark 4, then grease 3 baking sheets. Place the butter, granulated sugar and muscovado sugar in a bowl and beat until light and fluffy. Gradually beat in the egg and vanilla essence.

• Sift the flour, cocoa and bicarbonate of soda into the mixture and stir in carefully. Stir in the chocolate chips and walnuts. Drop dessertspoonfuls of the mixture on to the prepared baking sheets, spaced well apart to allow for spreading.

• Bake in the oven for 10–15 minutes, or until the mixture has spread and the cookies are beginning to feel firm.

• Remove from the oven, leave on the baking sheets for 2 minutes, then transfer to wire racks to cool completely.

MAKES 24

175 g/6 oz unsalted butter or
    margarine, plus extra
    for greasing

200 g/7 oz soft brown sugar

1 egg

70 g/2^1/$_2$ oz plain flour

1 tsp bicarbonate of soda

pinch of salt

70 g/2^1/$_2$ oz wholemeal flour

1 tbsp bran

225 g/8 oz plain chocolate chips

185 g/6^1/$_2$ oz rolled oats

1 tbsp strong coffee

100 g/3^1/$_2$ oz hazelnuts, toasted
    and chopped roughly

Chocolate and Coffee Wholemeal Cookies

These delicious dark biscuits, flavoured with coffee and toasted chopped hazelnuts, are perfect served with coffee.

• Preheat the oven to 190°C/375°F/Gas Mark 5. Grease 2 large baking sheets. Cream the butter and sugar together in a bowl. Add the egg and beat well, using a hand whisk if preferred.

• In a separate bowl, sieve together the plain flour, bicarbonate of soda and salt, then add in the wholemeal flour and bran. Mix in the egg mixture, then stir in the chocolate chips, oats, coffee and hazelnuts. Mix well, with an electric whisk if preferred.

• Put 24 rounded tablespoonfuls of the mixture on to the prepared baking sheets, allowing room for the biscuits to spread during cooking. Alternatively, with lightly floured hands, break off pieces of the mixture and roll into balls (about 25 g/1 oz each), place on the baking sheets and flatten them with the back of a teaspoon. Transfer the baking sheets to the preheated oven and bake for 16–18 minutes, or until the biscuits are golden brown.

• Remove from the oven, transfer the biscuits to a wire rack and leave to cool before serving.

MAKES 18–20

55 g/2 oz plain chocolate, broken
    into pieces
140 g/5 oz plain flour
1 tsp baking powder
1 egg
140 g/5 oz caster sugar
50 ml/2 fl oz sunflower oil, plus extra
    for oiling

1/2 tsp vanilla essence
2 tbsp icing sugar
1 small packet milk chocolate
    buttons (about 30 buttons)
1 small packet white chocolate
    buttons (about 30 buttons)

Black and White Cookies

These biscuits are topped with milk chocolate and white chocolate buttons, making them a favourite with children. Leave to cool completely before serving.

• Melt the plain chocolate in a heatproof bowl set over a saucepan of gently simmering water. Remove from the heat and leave to cool. Sieve the flour and baking powder together.

• Meanwhile, in a large bowl, whisk the egg, sugar, oil and vanilla essence together. Whisk in the cooled, melted chocolate until well blended, then gradually stir in the flour. Cover the bowl with clingfilm and refrigerate for at least 3 hours.

• Preheat the oven to 190°C/375°F/Gas Mark 5. Oil 1–2 large baking sheets. Shape tablespoonfuls of the mixture into log shapes using your hands, each measuring about 5 cm/2 inches. Roll the logs generously in the icing sugar, then place on the prepared baking sheets, allowing room for the biscuits to spread during cooking.

• Bake the biscuits in the preheated oven for about 15 minutes, until firm. Remove from the oven, and place 3 chocolate buttons down the centre of each, alternating the colours. Transfer to a wire rack and leave to cool.

MAKES 20

115 g/4 oz unsalted butter,
   softened, plus extra
   for greasing
115 g/4 oz light muscovado sugar
1 egg
100 g/3 1/2 oz porridge oats
1 tbsp milk

1 tsp vanilla essence
125 g/4 1/2 oz plain flour
1 tbsp cocoa powder
1/2 tsp baking powder
175 g/6 oz plain chocolate,
   broken into pieces
175 g/6 oz milk chocolate,
   broken into pieces

Chocolate Chip Oaties

After baking, biscuits must be left on the baking sheet for 2 minutes, because this ensures they do not fall apart when transferred to a wire rack to cool.

• Preheat the oven to 180°C/350°F/Gas Mark 4. Grease 2 large baking sheets. Place the butter and sugar in a bowl and beat together with a wooden spoon until light and fluffy.
• Beat in the egg, then add the oats, milk and vanilla essence. Beat together until well blended. Sieve the flour, cocoa and baking powder into the mixture and stir. Stir in the chocolate pieces.
• Place dessertspoonfuls of the mixture on the prepared baking sheets and flatten slightly with a fork. Bake in the preheated oven for 15 minutes, or until slightly risen and firm. Remove from the oven, cool on the baking sheets for 2 minutes, then transfer to wire racks to cool completely.

MAKES 24

90 g/3¹/4 oz unsalted butter, plus
    extra for greasing

365 g/12¹/2 oz plain chocolate

1 tsp strong coffee

2 eggs

140 g/5 oz soft brown sugar

185 g/6¹/2 oz plain flour

¹/4 tsp baking powder

pinch of salt

2 tsp almond essence

85 g/3 oz Brazil nuts, chopped

85 g/3 oz hazelnuts, chopped

40 g/1¹/2 oz white chocolate

Chocolate Temptations

Piping white and dark chocolate lines over these biscuits gives them a touch of elegance and sophistication.

• Preheat the oven to 180°C/350°F/Gas Mark 4. Grease 1–2 large baking sheets. Put 225 g/8 oz of the plain chocolate with the butter and coffee into a heatproof bowl set over a saucepan of gently simmering water and heat until the chocolate is almost melted.

• Meanwhile, beat the eggs in a bowl until fluffy. Gradually whisk in the sugar until thick. Remove the chocolate from the heat and stir until smooth. Add to the egg mixture and stir until combined.

• Sieve the flour, baking powder and salt into a bowl, then stir into the chocolate mixture. Chop 85 g/3 oz of the remaining plain chocolate into pieces and stir into the mixture. Stir in the almond essence and chopped nuts.

• Put 24 tablespoonfuls of the mixture on to the baking sheet, transfer to the preheated oven and bake for 16 minutes. Remove from the oven and transfer to a wire rack to cool. To decorate, melt the remaining chocolate (plain and white) in turn as in the first step, then spoon into a piping bag and pipe thin lines on to the biscuits.

MAKES 9

75 g/2³/4 oz unsalted butter or
    margarine, plus extra for greasing

225 g/8 oz plain chocolate
    digestive biscuits

200 ml/7 fl oz canned evaporated milk

1 egg, beaten

1 tsp vanilla essence

2 tbsp caster sugar

40 g/1¹/2 oz self-raising flour, sieved

125 g/4¹/2 oz grated coconut

50 g/1³/4 oz plain chocolate (optional)

Chocolate Coconut Layers

You can store the squares in an airtight container for up to 4 days. They can be frozen, undecorated, for up to 2 months. Defrost at room temperature.

• Preheat the oven to 190°C/375°F/Gas Mark 5. Grease a 20-cm/8-inch shallow, square cake tin and line the bottom with baking paper.

• Crush the biscuits in a polythene bag with a rolling pin or process them in a food processor. Melt the butter in a saucepan and stir in the crushed biscuits thoroughly. Remove from the heat and press the mixture into the bottom of the prepared cake tin.

• In a separate bowl, beat together the evaporated milk, egg, vanilla and sugar until smooth. Stir in the flour and grated coconut. Pour over the biscuit layer and use a palette knife to smooth the top.

• Bake in the preheated oven for 30 minutes, or until the coconut topping has become firm and just golden. Remove from the oven, leave to cool in the tin for about 5 minutes, then cut into squares. Leave to cool completely in the tin.

• Carefully remove the squares from the tin and place them on a chopping board. Melt the plain chocolate (if using) and drizzle it over the squares to decorate them. Leave the chocolate to set before serving.

MAKES 9
115 g/4 oz unsalted butter,
   plus extra for greasing
225 g/8 oz white chocolate

75 g/2¾ oz walnut pieces
2 eggs
115 g/4 oz soft brown sugar
115 g/4 oz self-raising flour

White Chocolate Brownies

You can vary the nuts in this recipe by using almonds, pecans or hazelnuts instead of the walnuts.

• Preheat the oven to 180°C/350°F/Gas Mark 4. Lightly grease an 18-cm/7-inch square cake tin.
• Coarsely chop 6 squares of white chocolate and all the walnuts. Put the remaining chocolate and the butter in a heatproof bowl set over a pan of gently simmering water. When melted, stir together, then set aside to cool slightly.
• Whisk the eggs and sugar together, then beat in the cooled chocolate mixture until well mixed. Fold in the flour, chopped chocolate and the walnuts. Turn the mixture into the prepared tin and smooth the surface.
• Transfer the tin to the preheated oven and bake for about 30 minutes, until just set. The mixture should still be a little soft in the centre. Remove from the oven, leave to cool in the tin, then cut into 9 squares before serving.

MAKES 20

85 g/3 oz unsalted butter, plus extra
    for greasing
100 g/3¹/2 oz demerara sugar
1 egg
25 g/1 oz wheatgerm

125 g/4¹/2 oz wholemeal
    self-raising flour
6 tbsp self-raising flour, sifted
125 g/4¹/2 oz plain chocolate,
    broken into pieces

Chocolate Wheatmeals

These biscuits can be frozen very successfully. Freeze them after they have cooled completely but before dipping in the melted chocolate. Thaw, dip them in melted chocolate, then leave to set before serving.

• Preheat the oven to 180°C/350°F/Gas Mark 4. Grease 1–2 baking sheets. Beat the butter and sugar in a bowl until fluffy. Add the egg and beat well. Stir in the wheatgerm and flours. Bring the mixture together with your hands.

• Roll rounded teaspoons of the mixture into balls and place on the prepared baking sheet or sheets, spaced well apart to allow for spreading. Flatten the biscuits slightly with a fork, then bake in the preheated oven for 15–20 minutes, or until golden.

• Remove from the oven and leave to cool on the baking sheets for a few minutes before transferring to a wire rack to cool completely.

• Melt the chocolate in a heatproof bowl set over a saucepan of gently simmering water, then dip each biscuit in the chocolate to cover the base and a little way up the sides. Let the excess chocolate drip back into the bowl. Place the biscuits on a sheet of baking paper and leave to set in a cool place before serving.

MAKES 16
55 g/2 oz unsalted butter,
    plus extra for greasing
55 g/2 oz caster sugar
115 g/4 oz plain flour

175 g/6 oz icing sugar
1–2 tbsp warm water
1/2 tsp peppermint essence
175 g/6 oz plain chocolate,
    broken into pieces

Chocolate Peppermint Slices

Take care when measuring the peppermint essence and do not hold the spoon directly over the bowl. If you add more than you intend and it splashes into the icing sugar mixture, you may find the topping too hot to handle.

• Preheat the oven to 180°C/350°F/Gas Mark 4. Grease and line a 20 x 30-cm/8 x 12-inch Swiss roll tin with baking paper. Beat the butter and caster sugar together until pale and fluffy. Stir in the flour until the mixture binds together.

• Knead the mixture to form a smooth dough, then press into the prepared tin. Prick the surface all over with a fork. Bake in the preheated oven for 10–15 minutes, until lightly browned and just firm to the touch. Remove from the oven and leave to cool in the tin.

• Sieve the icing sugar into a bowl. Gradually add the water, then add the peppermint essence. Spread the icing over the base, then leave to set.

• Melt the chocolate in a heatproof bowl set over a saucepan of gently simmering water, remove from the heat, then spread over the icing. Leave to set, then cut into slices.

MAKES 12

115 g/4 oz unsalted butter,
    plus extra for greasing
175 g/6 oz plain flour
55 g/2 oz golden caster sugar

FILLING AND TOPPING

175 g/6 oz butter
115 g/4 oz golden caster sugar
3 tbsp golden syrup
400 ml/14 fl oz canned
    condensed milk
200 g/7 oz plain chocolate,
    broken into pieces

Caramel Chocolate Shortbread

Take great care when cooking the caramel filling because it can very easily catch and burn on the base of the saucepan. Stir the mixture constantly until it has thickened.

• Preheat the oven to 180°C/350°F/Gas Mark 4. Grease and line the base of a 23-cm/9-inch shallow square cake tin. Place the butter, flour and sugar in a food processor and process until they begin to bind together. Press the mixture into the prepared tin and smooth the top. Bake in the preheated oven for 20–25 minutes, or until golden.

• Meanwhile, make the filling. Place the butter, sugar, syrup and condensed milk in a saucepan and heat gently until the sugar has dissolved. Bring to the boil and simmer for 6–8 minutes, stirring constantly, until the mixture becomes very thick. Remove the shortbread base from the oven, pour over the filling and chill in the refrigerator until firm.

• To make the topping, melt the chocolate in a heatproof bowl set over a saucepan of gently simmering water. Remove from the heat, leave to cool slightly, then spread over the caramel. Chill in the refrigerator until set. Cut it into 12 pieces with a sharp knife and serve.

Nuts are positive powerhouses of energy, so when you need a pick-me-up, whether with a well-earned morning mug of coffee or a restorative cup of tea in the afternoon, this chapter is packed with just what the doctor ordered. The cookies and bars in this chapter are great for lunch boxes for the children, too — especially because with homemade cookies, you choose just how much sugar and salt you want to include. A pecan cookie or a bar of hazelnut crunch, served with a glass of milk or fruit juice, will also satisfy after-school hunger pangs. In this chapter almonds, hazelnuts, pecans and walnuts are matched with tasty combinations of oats, spices, chocolate, syrup, fruit and even coffee to produce delicious nibbles for any time of day when you fancy a nourishing snack. And what could be nicer than homemade biscuits served with dessert at the end of a dinner party?

NUTTY BUT NICE

Nuts have a short storage life and can turn rancid very rapidly. Therefore it is best to buy them in fairly small quantities, as and when you need them, and store them in airtight containers in a cool, dark place. In any case, keep an eye on the 'use-by' date on the packaging. For best results, buy nuts in their shells and crack them open when you want to use them. Although this is time-consuming, the flavour and texture will be much better than using ready-shelled nuts. Discard any nuts with signs of mould on the shells or kernels, for not only will these taste horrible, spoiling all your hard work mixing in the cookie dough, they may contain toxins, which can cause unpleasant or even serious illness.

MAKES 9
115 g/4 oz unsalted butter,
    plus extra for greasing
225 g/8 oz soft brown sugar
1 egg

1 egg yolk
140 g/5 oz self-raising flour
1 tsp ground cinnamon
85 g/3 oz walnuts,
    roughly chopped

Walnut and Cinnamon Blondies

Do not chop the walnuts too finely, because the blondies should have a good texture and a slight crunch to them.

• Preheat the oven to 180°C/350°F/Gas Mark 4. Grease and line the base and sides of an 18-cm/7-inch square cake tin. Place the butter and sugar in a saucepan over a low heat and stir until the sugar has dissolved. Cook, stirring, for 1 minute more. The mixture will bubble slightly, but do not let it boil. Leave to cool for 10 minutes.

• Stir the egg and egg yolk into the mixture. Sift in the flour and cinnamon, then add the nuts and stir until just blended. Pour the cake mixture into the prepared pan and bake in the preheated oven for 20–25 minutes, or until springy in the middle and a toothpick inserted into the centre comes out clean.

• Leave to cool in the tin for a few minutes, then run a knife around the edge of the tin to loosen. Turn out on to a wire rack and peel off the paper. Leave to cool completely. When cold, cut into squares.

MAKES 15
115 g/4 oz unsalted butter, softened,
    plus extra for greasing
85 g/3 oz light muscovado sugar
1 egg, beaten

55 g/2 oz pecan nuts,
    chopped
85 g/3 oz plain flour
1/2 tsp baking powder
55 g/2 oz porridge oats

Oatie Pecan Cookies

To save a lot of hard work, beat the butter and sugar together with an electric hand-held mixer. Alternatively, use a food processor.

• Preheat the oven to 180°C/350°F/Gas Mark 4, then grease 2 baking sheets. Place the butter and sugar in a bowl and beat until light and fluffy. Gradually beat in the egg, then stir in the nuts.

• Sieve the flour and baking powder into the mixture and add the oats. Stir together until well combined. Drop dessertspoonfuls of the mixture on to the prepared baking sheets, spaced well apart to allow for spreading.

• Bake in the preheated oven for 15 minutes, or until pale golden. Remove from the oven, leave to cool on the baking sheets for 2 minutes, then transfer to wire racks to cool completely.

MAKES 8

3 eggs

60 g/2¼ oz ground almonds

140 g/5 oz milk powder

200 g/7 oz granulated sugar

½ tsp saffron threads

115 g/4 oz unsalted butter

1 tbsp flaked almonds, to decorate

Almond Slices

These almond slices are best eaten hot, but they may also be served cold. They can be made a day or even a week in advance and reheated. They also freeze beautifully.

• Preheat the oven to 160°C/325°F/Gas Mark 3. Lightly beat the eggs together in a mixing bowl and set aside.

• Place the ground almonds, milk powder, sugar and saffron in a large mixing bowl and stir to mix well.

• Melt the butter in a small saucepan over a low heat. Pour the melted butter over the dry ingredients and mix well with a wooden spoon until thoroughly combined.

• Add the beaten eggs to the mixture and stir to blend well.

• Spread the mixture evenly in a shallow 20-cm/8-inch ovenproof dish and bake in the preheated oven for 45 minutes, or until a cocktail stick inserted into the centre comes out clean.

• Remove from the oven and cut into slices. Decorate the slices with flaked almonds and transfer to serving plates. Serve hot or cold.

MAKES 30

175 g/6 oz unsalted butter or
    margarine, plus extra
    for greasing
225 g/8 oz demerara sugar
1 egg, beaten
4 tbsp milk
1 tsp vanilla essence

1/2 tsp almond essence
115 g/4 oz hazelnuts
140 g/5 oz plain flour
1 1/2 tsp ground mixed spice
1/4 tsp bicarbonate of soda
pinch of salt
300 g/10 1/2 oz porridge oats
150 g/5 1/2 oz sultanas

Oat and Hazelnut Morsels

Try these delicious biscuits with a refreshing cup of mint tea in the afternoon, or give them to hungry children as a snack.

• Preheat the oven to 190°C/375°F/Gas Mark 5. Grease 2 large baking sheets.
• Cream the butter and sugar together in a large mixing bowl. Blend in the egg, milk and vanilla and almond essences until thoroughly combined. Chop the hazelnuts finely.
• In a separate bowl, sieve the flour, mixed spice, bicarbonate of soda and salt together. Add to the creamed mixture slowly, stirring constantly. Mix in the oats, sultanas and hazelnuts.
• Put 30 rounded tablespoonfuls of the mixture on to the prepared baking sheets, spaced well apart to allow for spreading. Transfer to the preheated oven and bake for 12–15 minutes, or until the biscuits are golden brown.
• Remove the biscuits from the oven and place on a wire rack to cool before serving.

MAKES 20

225 g/8 oz unsalted butter, plus extra
   for greasing
70 g/2^1/$_2$ oz plain chocolate
125 g/4^1/$_2$ oz plain flour
^{3}/$_4$ tsp bicarbonate of soda

^{1}/$_4$ tsp baking powder
55 g/2 oz pecan nuts
100 g/3^1/$_2$ oz demerara sugar
^{1}/$_2$ tsp almond essence
1 egg
1 tsp milk

Pecan Brownies

Pecan nuts are very similar to walnuts, which you can substitute if you prefer.

• Preheat the oven to 180°C/350°F/Gas Mark 4. Grease a large baking dish and line it with baking paper.
• Put the chocolate in a heatproof bowl set over a saucepan of gently simmering water and heat until it is melted. Meanwhile, sieve together the flour, bicarbonate of soda and baking powder into a large bowl.
• Finely chop the pecan nuts and set aside. In a separate bowl, cream together the butter and sugar, then mix in the almond essence and the egg. Remove the chocolate from the heat and stir into the butter mixture. Add the flour mixture, milk and chopped nuts to the bowl and stir until well combined.
• Spoon the mixture into the prepared baking dish and smooth it. Transfer to the preheated oven and cook for 30 minutes, or until firm to the touch (it should still be a little soft in the centre). Remove from the oven and leave to cool completely. Cut into 20 squares and serve.

MAKES ABOUT 60
150 g/5¹/2 oz unsalted butter, at
    room temperature, plus extra
    for greasing
150 g/5¹/2 oz caster sugar
115 g/4 oz plain flour

25 g/1 oz ground almonds
pinch of salt
75 g/2³/4 oz blanched almonds, lightly
    toasted and finely chopped
finely grated rind of 1 large lemon
4 egg whites

Almond Biscuits

You can toast almonds by dry-frying them in a heavy-based frying pan or by spreading them out on a baking sheet and placing in a preheated oven, 180°C/350°F/Gas Mark 4. They take only a few minutes and it's important to watch them carefully because they burn easily.

• Preheat the oven to 180°C/350°F/Gas Mark 4. Grease 2 baking sheets. Put the butter and sugar into a bowl and beat until light and fluffy. Sieve over the flour, ground almonds and salt, tipping in any ground almonds left in the sieve. Use a large metal spoon to fold in the chopped almonds and grated lemon rind.
• In a separate, grease-free bowl, whisk the egg whites until soft peaks form. Fold these into the almond mixture.
• Drop small teaspoonfuls of the biscuit mixture on to the prepared baking sheets, spacing them very well apart to allow for spreading. (You might need to cook in batches.) Bake in a preheated oven for 15–20 minutes until golden brown around the edges. Remove from the oven and transfer to a wire rack to cool completely. Continue baking until all the mixture is used. Store the biscuits in an airtight container for up to 1 week.

MAKES 18
225 g/8 oz unsalted butter,
    plus extra for greasing
115 g/4 oz walnut pieces
175 g/6 oz caster sugar

2–3 drops vanilla essence
225 g/8 oz plain flour
200 g/7 oz plain chocolate chips

Walnut and Chocolate Chip Slices

Unsalted butter is always better for baking sweet treats. It's also ideal for greasing because it is less likely to burn than salted butter. An alternative is to brush the baking sheet with a bland oil, such as sunflower.

• Preheat the oven to 180°C/350°F/Gas Mark 4. Grease a 20 x 30-cm/8 x 12-inch Swiss roll tin. Coarsely chop the walnut pieces to about the same size as the chocolate chips.

• Beat the butter and sugar together until pale and fluffy. Add the vanilla essence, then stir in the flour. Stir in the walnuts and chocolate chips. Press the mixture into the prepared tin. Bake the mixture in the preheated oven for 20–25 minutes until golden brown. Remove from the oven, cool in the tin, then cut into slices.

MAKES ABOUT 16

115 g/4 oz unsalted butter, softened,
    plus extra for greasing
115 g/4 oz light muscovado sugar
85 g/3 oz golden granulated sugar
1 tsp vanilla essence
1 tbsp instant coffee granules,
    dissolved in 1 tbsp hot water

1 egg
175 g/6 oz plain flour
1/2 tsp baking powder
1/4 tsp bicarbonate of soda
55 g/2 oz milk chocolate chips
55 g/2 oz shelled walnuts,
    roughly chopped

Mocha Walnut Cookies

Muscovado sugar has a tendency to be quite lumpy, so it is a good idea to sieve it before use when baking cakes and biscuits.

• Preheat the oven to 180°C/350°F/Gas Mark 4. Grease 2 large baking sheets with a little butter. Place the butter, muscovado sugar and granulated sugar in a large bowl and beat together thoroughly until light and fluffy. Place the vanilla essence, coffee and egg in a separate large bowl and whisk together.

• Gradually add the coffee mixture to the butter and sugar, beating until fluffy. Sieve the flour, baking powder and bicarbonate of soda into the mixture and fold in carefully. Fold in the chocolate chips and walnuts.

• Drop dessertspoonfuls of the mixture on to the prepared baking sheets, spacing well apart to allow room for spreading. Bake in the preheated oven for 10–15 minutes, or until crisp on the outside but still soft inside. Remove from the oven, cool on the baking sheets for 2 minutes, then transfer to wire racks to cool completely.

MAKES 12
115 g/4 oz unsalted butter,
  plus extra for greasing
200 g/7 oz rolled oats
55 g/2 oz hazelnuts, lightly toasted
  and chopped

55 g/2 oz plain flour
85 g/3 oz light muscovado sugar
2 tbsp golden syrup
55 g/2 oz plain chocolate chips

Hazelnut Chocolate Crunch

Heat the butter, sugar and syrup in a microwave oven on Medium for 2¹/₂ minutes, instead of using a saucepan.

• Preheat the oven to 180°C/350°F/Gas Mark 4. Grease a 23-cm/9-inch shallow, square baking tin. Mix the oats, nuts and flour in a large bowl.
• Place the butter, sugar and syrup in a large saucepan and heat gently until the sugar has dissolved. Pour in the dry ingredients and mix well. Stir in the chocolate chips.
• Turn the mixture into the prepared tin and bake in the preheated oven for 20–25 minutes, or until golden brown and firm to the touch. Using a knife, mark into 12 rectangles and leave to cool in the tin. Cut the hazelnut chocolate crunch bars with a sharp knife before carefully removing them from the tin.

MAKES 24

200 g/7 oz unsalted butter,
    plus extra for greasing
275 g/9¹/2 oz demerara sugar
1 egg
140 g/5 oz plain flour, sieved
1 tsp baking powder

1 tsp bicarbonate of soda
125 g/4¹/2 oz porridge oats
1 tbsp bran
1 tbsp wheatgerm
115 g/4 oz mixed nuts,
    toasted and roughly chopped
200 g/7 oz plain chocolate chips

115 g/4 oz raisins and sultanas
175 g/6 oz plain chocolate,
    roughly chopped

Nutty Drizzles

Porridge oats are also sometimes labelled oatflakes or rolled oats (but not oatmeal).

• Preheat the oven to 180°C/350°F/Gas Mark 4. Grease 2 large baking sheets. In a large bowl, cream together the butter, sugar and egg. Add the flour, baking powder, bicarbonate of soda, oats, bran and wheatgerm and mix together until well combined. Finally, stir in the nuts, chocolate chips and dried fruit.

• Put 24 rounded tablespoonfuls of the mixture on to the prepared baking sheets. Transfer to the preheated oven and bake for 12 minutes, or until the biscuits are golden brown.

• Remove the biscuits from the oven, then transfer to a wire rack and leave to cool. Meanwhile, heat the chocolate pieces in a heatproof bowl set over a saucepan of gently simmering water until melted. Stir the chocolate, then leave to cool slightly. Use a spoon to drizzle the chocolate in waves over the biscuits, or spoon it into a piping bag and pipe zigzag lines over the biscuits. When the chocolate has set, store the biscuits in an airtight container in the refrigerator until ready to serve.

Nutritionists recommend that we eat five portions of fruit and vegetables a day, but this is not always practical and can prove to be quite a problem, especially if you have fussy eaters in your household. The scrumptious nibbles in this chapter include apricots, figs, cherries, dates, currants, raisins, sultanas and bananas, combined with a mouth-watering range of other ingredients as varied as nuts, seeds, oats, honey, spices, chocolate and fruit juice. They are sure to be a runaway success with every member of the family — and, of course, there is no need for you to tell anyone that these tasty snacks are actually quite healthy too.

Fruit bars are ideal for the school lunch box and can also provide a kick-start to the day for busy adults who have no time for breakfast. They make a great pick-me-up whenever your energy is flagging and are the perfect after-school snack for kids.

FRUITFUL ENDEAVOURS

From Apricot Flapjacks to Caribbean Cookies, the recipes in this chapter are easy to follow, quick and economical, so there is no excuse for not having a ready supply of tasty treats to hand. Furthermore, many of the ingredients for these cookies and bars are storecupboard staples, such as honey, porridge oats and dried fruit. It is easy to substitute one kind of dried fruit for another — dates instead of figs or sultanas instead of raisins — so you can customize your baking to your resources and, more importantly, to your family's tastes. Do keep an eye on the 'use-by' dates on the packets to ensure that your biscuits have the best and freshest flavour.

MAKES 10
sunflower oil, for oiling
175 g/6 oz polyunsaturated spread
85 g/3 oz demerara sugar
clear honey

140 g/5 oz ready-to-eat dried
apricots, chopped
2 tsp sesame seeds
225 g/8 oz porridge oats

Apricot Flapjacks

Ready-to-eat dried apricots are ideal for this recipe, because they do not need soaking. You could use dried figs, dates or muscatel raisins for a change of flavour.

• Preheat the oven to 180°C/350°F/Gas Mark 4. Very lightly oil a 26 x 17-cm/10½ x 6½-inch shallow cake tin.
• Put the spread, sugar and honey into a small saucepan over a low heat and heat until the ingredients have melted together — do not allow the mixture to boil. When the ingredients are warm and well combined, stir in the apricots, sesame seeds and oats.
• Spoon the mixture into the prepared tin and lightly level with the back of a spoon. Cook in the preheated oven for 20–25 minutes or until golden brown. Remove from the oven, cut into 10 bars and leave to cool completely before removing from the cake tin. Store the flapjacks in an airtight container and consume within 2–3 days.

MAKES 20

225 g/8 oz unsalted butter or
    margarine, plus extra
    for greasing
75 g/2³/4 oz dried figs
115 g/4 oz clear honey
4 tbsp demerara sugar

2 eggs, beaten
pinch of salt
1 tsp mixed spice
1 tsp bicarbonate of soda
½ tsp vanilla essence
2 tbsp dried dates,
    finely chopped

225 g/8 oz plain flour
175 g/6 oz porridge oats
40 g/1½ oz walnuts,
    finely chopped
dried fig pieces,
    to decorate (optional)

Fig and Walnut Biscuits

When making cream mixtures, remove the butter from the refrigerator about 30 minutes before you need to use it to let it come to room temperature and soften slightly.

• Preheat the oven to 180°C/350°F/Gas Mark 4. Grease 2 large baking sheets.
• Finely chop the figs. Mix the butter, honey, figs and sugar together in a large bowl. Beat the eggs into the mixture and mix thoroughly.
• In a separate bowl, combine the salt, mixed spice, bicarbonate of soda, vanilla essence and dates. Gradually stir them into the creamed mixture. Sieve the flour into the mixture and stir well. Finally, mix in the oats and walnuts.
• Drop 20 rounded tablespoonfuls of the mixture on to the prepared baking sheets, spaced well apart to allow for spreading. Decorate with fig pieces, if using. Bake in the preheated oven for 10–15 minutes, or until the biscuits are golden brown.
• Remove the biscuits from the oven, transfer to a wire rack and leave to cool before serving.

MAKES ABOUT 14

55 g/2 oz unsalted butter

40 g/1 1/2 oz demerara sugar

1 tbsp golden syrup

55 g/2 oz plain flour, sieved

25 g/1 oz angelica,
roughly chopped

25 g/1 oz glacé cherries,
roughly chopped

55 g/2 oz flaked almonds,
roughly chopped

55 g/2 oz glacé pineapple,
roughly chopped

1 tsp lemon juice

115 g/4 oz plain chocolate,
melted and cooled

Pineapple and Cherry Florentines

If you have difficulty removing the florentines from the baking sheet, return them to the oven for 2 minutes, then lift off and cool on a wire rack.

• Preheat the oven to 180°C/350°F/Gas Mark 4. Line 1 or 2 large baking sheets with non-stick baking paper. Place the butter, sugar and syrup in a saucepan and heat gently until melted, then stir in the flour, angelica, cherries, almonds, pineapple and lemon juice.

• Place walnut-sized mounds of the mixture spaced well apart on the prepared baking sheets and flatten gently with a fork. Bake in the preheated oven for 8–10 minutes, or until golden. Use a palette knife to neaten the ragged edges. Leave to cool for 1 minute, then transfer to a wire rack to cool completely.

• Spread the melted chocolate over the base of each florentine, placing the biscuits, chocolate side up, on a wire rack. Use a fork to mark the chocolate with wavy lines. Leave until set.

MAKES 36

125 g/4½ oz unsalted butter or
    margarine, plus extra for greasing
175 g/6 oz ready-to-eat dried apricots
85 g/3 oz dried dates
140 g/5 oz plain flour
75 g/2¾ oz porridge oats

90 g/3¼ oz wheat flakes
½ tsp bicarbonate of soda
pinch of salt
140 g/5 oz soft brown sugar,
    plus extra for dusting
2 eggs
1 tsp almond essence

Fruit Morsels

You can chop dried fruit with a heavy-bladed kitchen knife or snip it into pieces with a pair of strong kitchen scissors – whichever is easier.

• Preheat the oven to 190°C/375°F/Gas Mark 5. Grease 2 large baking sheets with butter. Chop the dried apricots and dates. Sift the flour into a large bowl and mix in the oats, wheat flakes, bicarbonate of soda and salt.

• In a separate bowl, blend together the sugar and butter. Beat in the eggs until the mixture is light and fluffy. Gradually add the flour mixture, stirring. Blend in the almond essence and fruit. Mix well.

• Drop 36 teaspoonfuls of the mixture on to the prepared baking sheets, spaced very well apart to allow for spreading. Dust with sugar. Bake for 10 minutes, or until golden brown.

• Remove the biscuits from the oven, place on a wire rack and leave them to cool before serving.

MAKES 24
175 g/6 oz unsalted butter, softened,
    plus extra for greasing
175 g/6 oz golden caster sugar
1 egg, beaten
2 tbsp milk

55 g/2 oz chopped mixed peel
115 g/4 oz currants
350 g/12 oz plain flour,
    plus extra for dusting
1 tsp mixed spice

GLAZE
1 egg white, lightly beaten
2 tbsp golden caster sugar

Easter Biscuits

Be careful when sprinkling the sugar over the glaze – any sugar sprinkled directly on to the baking sheet will burn on to its surface.

• Preheat the oven to 180°C/350°F/Gas Mark 4, then grease 2 large baking sheets. Place the butter and sugar in a bowl and beat until light and fluffy. Gradually beat in the egg and milk. Stir in the mixed peel and currants, then sieve in the flour and mixed spice. Mix together to make a firm dough. Knead lightly until smooth.
• On a floured work surface, roll out the dough to 5 mm/¼ inch thick and use a 5-cm/2-inch round biscuit cutter to stamp out the biscuits. Re-roll the dough trimmings and stamp out more biscuits until the dough is used up. Place the biscuits on the prepared baking sheets and bake in the preheated oven for 10 minutes.
• Remove from the oven to glaze. Brush with the egg white and sprinkle with the caster sugar, then return to the oven for a further 5 minutes, or until lightly browned. Leave to cool on the baking sheets for 2 minutes, then transfer to wire racks to cool completely.

MAKES 24
unsalted butter, for greasing
25 g/1 oz mashed banana
1 tbsp pineapple juice
1 tbsp orange juice
4 tbsp groundnut oil
1 egg

1 tbsp milk
140 g/5 oz plain flour
1/4 tsp bicarbonate of soda
75 g/2³/4 oz desiccated coconut
demerara sugar, for sprinkling

Caribbean Cookies

If you prefer, substitute grated fresh coconut for the desiccated. You could also use finely chopped, very ripe mango instead of the mashed banana.

• Preheat the oven to 180°C/350°F/Gas Mark 4. Grease a large baking sheet.
• In a large bowl, cream together the banana, fruit juices, oil, egg and milk. Transfer the mixture to a food mixer. With the machine running, sieve in the flour and bicarbonate of soda, beating constantly. Add the desiccated coconut and mix well.
• Drop rounded teaspoonfuls on to the prepared baking sheet, spaced well apart to allow for spreading. Sprinkle with the demerara sugar, then transfer to the preheated oven and bake for about 10 minutes, or until the cookies are golden brown.
• Remove the cookies from the oven and transfer to a wire rack to cool before serving.

MAKES 9

115 g/4 oz unsalted butter,
    plus extra for greasing
2 tbsp clear honey
1 egg, beaten
85 g/3 oz ground almonds

115 g/4 oz ready-to-eat dried
    apricots, finely chopped
55 g/2 oz dried cherries
55 g/2 oz toasted hazelnuts
25 g/1 oz sesame seeds
85 g/3 oz jumbo oats

Fruit and Nut Squares

The easiest way to smooth the surface of the mixture is with the back of a slightly damp tablespoon or a damp palette knife. Smoothing the surface ensures that the mixture bakes through and is an even golden brown.

• Preheat the oven to 180°C/350°F/Gas Mark 4. Lightly grease an 18-cm/7-inch shallow, square cake tin with butter. Beat the remaining butter with the honey in a bowl until creamy, then beat in the egg with the almonds.
• Add the remaining ingredients and mix together well. Press into the prepared tin, ensuring that the mixture is firmly packed. Smooth the top.
• Transfer to the preheated oven and bake for 20–25 minutes, or until firm to the touch and golden brown.
• Remove from the oven and leave to stand for 10 minutes before marking into squares. Leave until cold before removing from the tin. Cut into squares and store in an airtight container.

MAKES 30

175 g/6 oz unsalted butter or
    margarine, plus extra for greasing
200 g/7 oz soft brown sugar
2 eggs
350 g/12 oz plain flour
pinch of salt
2 tsp baking powder
2 tbsp milk

1 tsp almond essence
150 g/5½ oz chopped walnuts
75 g/2¾ oz raisins
75 g/2¾ oz sultanas
100 g/3½ oz maraschino cherries
200 g/7 oz wheat flakes, crushed
15 maraschino cherries, halved,
    to decorate

Cherry and Walnut Biscuits

The slightly bitter flavour of maraschino cherries gives these biscuits an intriguing flavour. However, you could use sweet cherries if you prefer.

• Preheat the oven to 190°C/375°F/Gas Mark 5. Grease 1 or 2 large baking sheets.
• Cream the butter and sugar in a large mixing bowl until the mixture is light and fluffy. Beat in the eggs.
• Gradually sieve the flour, salt and baking powder into the creamed mixture. Add the milk and almond essence and mix thoroughly. Stir in the walnuts, dried fruit and maraschino cherries.
• Form the dough into 30 balls (about 1 rounded tablespoon each) and roll in the crushed wheat flakes. Place the dough balls on the prepared baking sheet, spaced about 2.5 cm/1 inch apart. Place half a maraschino cherry on the top of each dough ball. Transfer to the preheated oven and cook for 10 minutes, or until the biscuits are light brown. Transfer from the oven to a wire rack and leave to cool completely before serving.

MAKES 16
200 g/7 oz unsalted butter,
    plus extra for greasing
200 g/7 oz demerara sugar
2 tbsp golden syrup

275 g/9^1/$_2$ oz porridge oats
100 g/3^1/$_2$ oz desiccated coconut
75 g/2^3/$_4$ oz glacé cherries, chopped

Coconut Flapjacks

Store flapjacks in an airtight container and eat within 1 week. They can also be frozen for up to 1 month.

• Preheat the oven to 160°C/325°F/Gas Mark 3. Grease a 30 x 23-cm/12 x 9-inch baking tray.
• Put the butter, sugar and syrup in a large saucepan and set over a low heat until just melted. Stir in the oats, coconut and cherries and mix until evenly combined.
• Spread the mixture evenly on to the baking tray and press down with the back of a spatula or palette knife to make a smooth surface.
• Bake in the preheated oven for 30 minutes. Remove from the oven and leave to cool on the baking tray for 10 minutes. Using a sharp knife, cut the flapjack into rectangles. Carefully transfer the pieces of flapjack to a wire rack and leave to cool completely.

MAKES 16

225 g/8 oz plain flour

1 tsp baking powder

100 g/3½ oz caster sugar

85 g/3 oz soft brown sugar

225 g/8 oz unsalted butter

150 g/5½ oz porridge oats

225 g/8 oz strawberry jam

100 g/3½ oz plain chocolate chips

25 g/1 oz almonds, chopped

Strawberry and Chocolate Slices

Other flavours of jam also go well with chocolate. Raspberry is a classic partner, but you may want to sieve out any pips before spreading it over the cooked base.

• Preheat the oven to 190°C/375°F/Gas Mark 5. Line a 30 x 20-cm/12 x 8-inch deep-sided Swiss roll tin with baking paper. Sieve the flour and baking powder into a large bowl.

• Add the caster sugar and brown sugar to the flour and mix well. Add the butter and rub in until the mixture resembles breadcrumbs. Stir in the oats.

• Press three-quarters of the mixture into the base of the prepared cake tin. Bake in the preheated oven for 10 minutes.

• Spread the jam over the cooked base, then sprinkle over the chocolate chips. Mix the remaining flour mixture with the almonds. Sprinkle evenly over the chocolate chips and press down gently.

• Return to the oven and bake for a further 20–25 minutes until golden brown. Remove from the oven, leave to cool in the tin, then cut into slices.

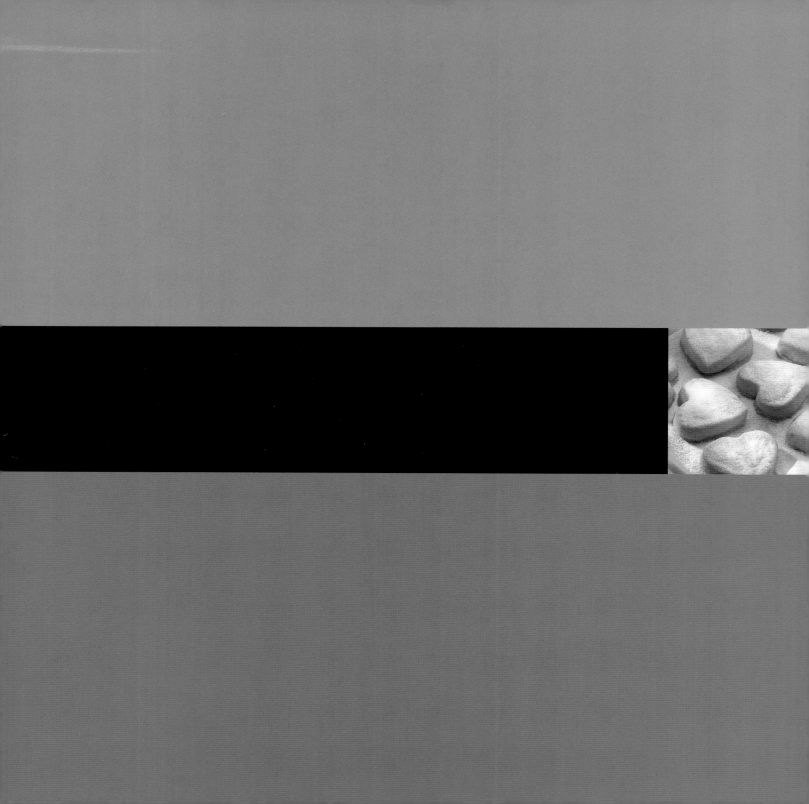

All homemade cookies and bars are special, but the ones in this chapter have that little something extra, whether charming, dainty Vanilla Hearts – perfect for a wedding anniversary morning tea tray – or Lavender Biscuits – the epitome of elegance for a sunny tea party on the lawn.

Lots of occasions call for a special treat, and in this chapter you are sure to find a delicious but easy recipe for just the right tempting little snack, whether for a fund-raising coffee morning, a tea tray to welcome new neighbours, a school summer fair or just to spoil the family. Homemade biscuits also make delightful presents, especially if you pack them in an attractive box or wrap them in cellophane tied with a colourful ribbon. You could even give a delicate cup and saucer packed with special biscuits.

SOMETHING SPECIAL

Many of the biscuits in this chapter are also wonderful accompaniments to creamy desserts and ice-cream, adding a subtle but impressive flourish to any formal dinner party. And, of course, Amaretti, those crunchy, almond-flavoured, moreish morsels from Italy, are traditionally served to guests with a glass of chilled white wine, whatever the time of day.

Allow just a little more time for the recipes in this chapter, mainly because most of the biscuits have extra decoration, so you will need time for them to cool and for icing or melted chocolate to set. However, you are sure to find that this little extra effort is well worth it when you see how fast the biscuits disappear from the plate.

MAKES 16
175 g/6 oz unsalted butter,
    plus extra for greasing
225 g/8 oz plain flour
1 tsp ground ginger
85 g/3 oz golden caster sugar

GINGER TOPPING
1 tbsp golden syrup
55 g/2 oz unsalted butter
2 tbsp icing sugar
1 tsp ground ginger

WHITE ICING (OPTIONAL)
125 g/4¹/₂ oz icing sugar
1 tbsp milk

Ginger-Topped Fingers

The shortbread base will be quite soft when it first comes out of the oven, but it will become firm as it cools. These biscuits are best left to cool completely before serving.

• Preheat the oven to 180°C/350°F/Gas Mark 4. Grease a 28 x 18-cm/11 x 7-inch rectangular cake tin. Sieve the flour and ginger into a bowl and stir in the sugar. Rub in the butter until the mixture resembles a dough.
• Press the mixture into the prepared tin and smooth the top with a palette knife. Bake in the preheated oven for 40 minutes, or until very lightly browned.
• To make the ginger topping, place the syrup and butter in a small saucepan over a low heat and stir until melted. Stir in the icing sugar and ginger. Remove the biscuit base from the oven and pour over the topping while hot. Leave to cool slightly in the tin, then cut into 16 fingers. Transfer to wire racks to cool completely.
• To make the icing (if using), mix the icing sugar with the milk until smooth. Pour it into a piping bag with a thin nozzle, and pipe thin parallel lines lengthways on top of each finger. Drag a cocktail stick or a tip of a knife crossways through the lines, alternately towards you then away from you, about 1 cm/½ inch apart, to create a wavy effect.

MAKES 12

125 g/4¹/2 oz unsalted butter,
    softened
75 g/2³/4 oz golden icing sugar
125 g/4¹/2 oz plain flour
40 g/1¹/2 oz cocoa powder
¹/2 tsp ground cinnamon

FILLING

125 g/4¹/2 oz plain chocolate,
    broken into pieces
50 ml/2 fl oz double cream

Cookies and Cream Sandwiches

Do not sandwich the biscuits together too long before serving, otherwise they will go soft. Store unsandwiched biscuits in an airtight container for up to 3 days.

• Preheat the oven to 160°C/325°F/Gas Mark 3. Line a baking sheet with non-stick baking paper. Place the butter and sugar in a large bowl and beat together until light and fluffy. Sieve the flour, cocoa powder and ground cinnamon into the bowl and mix until a smooth dough forms.

• Place the dough between 2 sheets of non-stick baking paper and roll out to 3 mm/¹/8 inch thick. Stamp out 6-cm/2¹/2-inch rounds and place on the prepared baking sheet. Bake in the preheated oven for 15 minutes, or until firm to the touch. Leave to cool for 2 minutes, then transfer to wire racks to cool completely.

• To make the filling, place the chocolate and cream in a saucepan and heat gently until the chocolate has melted. Stir until smooth. Leave to cool, then leave to chill in the refrigerator for 2 hours, or until firm. Sandwich the biscuits together in pairs with a spoonful of chocolate cream and serve.

MAKES ABOUT 40
150 g/5¹/₂ oz blanched almonds
150 g/5¹/₂ oz caster sugar
1 large egg white
icing sugar, for dusting

Amaretti

To intensify the almond flavour, add a drop or two of almond essence with the egg white. This is the secret of the popular *Amaretti di Saronno*. You could also wrap individual biscuits in colourful tissue paper if you are planning to give them as a gift.

• Preheat the oven to 120°C/250°F/Gas Mark ½. Use a pestle and mortar to crush the almonds with the caster sugar, or finely chop the almonds and then combine with the sugar in a bowl.
• Lightly beat the egg white, then stir it into the almond mixture to form a firm dough. Line 2 large baking sheets with baking paper and place walnut-sized portions of the dough on them, spaced well apart to allow for spreading. Dust with icing sugar. Bake in the preheated oven for 30 minutes. Remove from the oven and transfer to wire racks to cool completely.

MAKES 40

225 g/8 oz unsalted butter, softened,
    plus extra for greasing

55 g/2 oz golden caster sugar

225 g/8 oz plain flour

115 g/4 oz cornflour

1 tsp ground cinnamon

55 g/2 oz sieved icing sugar,
    to decorate

Mexican Pastelitos

These biscuits are traditionally made in this small size, but you could make larger biscuits, if you prefer.

• Preheat the oven to 160°C/325°F/Gas Mark 3. Grease 2 baking sheets. Place the butter and caster sugar in a bowl and beat until light and fluffy. Sieve the flour, cornflour and cinnamon into a separate bowl, then gradually work them into the creamed mixture with a wooden spoon. When well mixed, knead until smooth.

• Take 1 teaspoon at a time of the mixture and roll into a ball. Place the little balls on the prepared baking sheets. Bake in the preheated oven for 30–40 minutes, or until pale golden.

• Place the icing sugar in a shallow dish and toss the pastelitos in it while they are still warm. Leave to cool on wire racks.

MAKES ABOUT 30
115 g/4 oz unsalted butter, softened,
    plus extra for greasing
55 g/2 oz golden icing sugar, sieved
125 g/4½ oz plain flour

1 tbsp cocoa powder
100 g/3½ oz plain chocolate,
    melted and cooled

Chocolate Viennese Fingers

Sprinkle some chopped
nuts on to the chocolate-
coated ends of these
biscuits while the chocolate
is still soft, if you like.

• Preheat the oven to 180°C/350°F/Gas Mark 4. Grease 2 large baking sheets. Beat the butter and sugar together until light and fluffy. Sieve the flour and cocoa powder into the bowl and work the mixture until it is a smooth, piping consistency.
• Spoon into a large piping bag fitted with a 2.5-cm/1-inch star nozzle. Pipe 6-cm/2½-inch lengths of the mixture on to the prepared baking sheets, spacing them well apart to allow for spreading. Bake in the preheated oven for 15 minutes, or until firm.
• Remove from the oven and leave to cool on the baking sheets for 2 minutes, then transfer to a wire rack to cool completely. Dip the ends of the biscuits into the melted chocolate and leave to set before serving.

MAKES 12
150 g/5½ oz unsalted butter,
    cut into small pieces,
    plus extra for greasing
225 g/8 oz plain flour,
    plus extra for dusting

125 g/4½ oz caster sugar,
    plus extra for dusting
1 tsp vanilla essence

Vanilla Hearts

Place a fresh vanilla pod in your caster sugar and keep it in a storage jar for several weeks to give the sugar a delicious vanilla flavour.

• Preheat the oven to 180°C/350°F/Gas Mark 4. Lightly grease a large baking sheet. Sieve the flour into a large bowl. Add the butter and rub in with your fingertips until the mixture resembles fine breadcrumbs. Stir in the caster sugar and vanilla essence and mix together to form a firm dough.
• Roll out the dough on a lightly floured work surface to a thickness of 2.5 cm/1 inch. Stamp out 12 hearts with a heart-shaped biscuit cutter measuring about 5 cm/2 inches across and 2.5 cm/1 inch deep. Arrange the hearts on the prepared baking sheet.
• Transfer to the preheated oven and bake for 15–20 minutes, or until the hearts are a light golden colour. Transfer the vanilla hearts to a wire rack and leave to cool completely. Dust them with caster sugar just before serving.

MAKES 12

55 g/2 oz unsalted butter,
    plus extra for greasing
55 g/2 oz raisins
2 tbsp brandy
115 g/4 oz plain chocolate,
    broken into pieces
115 g/4 oz milk chocolate,
    broken into pieces

2 tbsp golden syrup
175 g/6 oz digestive biscuits,
    roughly broken
55 g/2 oz flaked almonds,
    lightly toasted
25 g/1 oz glacé cherries,
    chopped

TOPPING

100 g/3^1/$_2$ oz plain chocolate,
    broken into pieces
20 g/^{3}/$_4$ oz butter

Tiffin

For a decorative effect, use a fork to mark light wavy lines over the chocolate topping before leaving it to set in the refrigerator.

• Grease and line the base of an 18-cm/7-inch shallow, square cake tin. Place the raisins and brandy in a bowl and leave to soak for about 30 minutes. Put the chocolate, butter and syrup in a saucepan and heat gently until melted.

• Stir in the digestive biscuits, almonds, cherries, raisins and brandy. Turn into the prepared tin and leave to cool. Cover and leave to chill in the refrigerator for 1 hour.

• To make the topping, place the chocolate and butter in a small heatproof bowl and set over a saucepan of gently simmering water until melted. Stir and pour over the biscuit base. Leave to chill in the refrigerator for 8 hours or overnight. Cut into bars or squares to serve.

MAKES 24
175 g/6 oz unsalted butter,
    plus extra for greasing
55 g/2 oz eating apple,
    cored and cooked
50 g/1³/4 oz soft brown sugar
5 tbsp molasses
1 egg white

1 tsp almond essence
200 g/7 oz plain flour
1/4 tsp bicarbonate of soda
1/4 tsp baking powder
pinch of salt
1/2 tsp mixed spice
1/2 tsp ground ginger

Gingerbread Squares

Mixed spice is exactly what it says on the label but you could substitute your own combination of spices, such as ground cinnamon, freshly grated nutmeg or mace and ground cloves.

• Preheat the oven to 180°C/350°F/Gas Mark 4. Grease a large cake tin and line it with baking paper. Chop the apple and set aside. Put the butter, sugar, molasses, egg white and almond essence in a food processor and process until the mixture is smooth.
• Sieve together the flour, bicarbonate of soda, baking powder, salt, mixed spice and ginger in another bowl. Add to the creamed mixture and beat together well until combined. Stir the apple into the mixture, then pour the mixture into the prepared cake tin.
• Transfer to the preheated oven and bake for 10 minutes, or until golden brown. Remove from the oven and cut into 24 pieces. Transfer the gingerbread to a wire rack and leave to cool completely before serving.

MAKES 20

140 g/5 oz unsalted butter

115 g/4 oz caster sugar

1 egg yolk

115 g/4 oz ground almonds

175 g/6 oz plain flour

55 g/2 oz plain chocolate,
     broken into pieces

2 tbsp icing sugar

2 tbsp cocoa powder

Ladies' Kisses

Place the dough balls well apart from each other on the baking sheets because they will spread out during cooking. You may need to cook the biscuits in batches.

• Line 3 baking sheets with baking paper or use non-stick sheets. Beat the butter and caster sugar together in a bowl until pale and fluffy. Beat in the egg yolk, then the almonds and flour. Continue beating until well mixed. Shape the dough into a ball, wrap in clingfilm and leave to chill in the refrigerator for 1½–2 hours.

• Preheat the oven to 160°C/325°F/Gas Mark 3. Unwrap the dough, break off walnut-sized pieces and roll them into balls between the palms of your hands. Place the dough balls on the prepared baking sheets, spaced well apart to allow for spreading. Bake in the preheated oven for 20–25 minutes, or until golden brown. Remove from the oven and carefully transfer the biscuits, still on the baking paper if using, to wire racks to cool.

• Place the plain chocolate in a small heatproof bowl set over a saucepan of gently simmering water, and stir constantly until melted. Remove the bowl from the heat. Remove the biscuits from the baking paper, if using, and spread the melted chocolate over the bases. Sandwich them together in pairs and return to the wire racks to cool and set. Dust with a mixture of sifted icing sugar and cocoa powder and serve.

MAKES 12
115 g/4 oz unsalted butter,
    softened, plus extra for greasing
55 g/2 oz golden caster sugar,
    plus extra for dusting

1 tsp chopped lavender leaves
finely grated rind of 1 lemon
175 g/6 oz plain flour

Lavender Biscuits

If you do not have a food processor, you can mix the dough by hand. Knead it into a ball before rolling the dough out.

• Preheat the oven to 150°C/300°F/Gas Mark 2, then grease a large baking sheet. Place the caster sugar and lavender leaves in a food processor. Process until the lavender is very finely chopped, then add the butter and lemon rind and process until light and fluffy. Transfer to a large bowl. Sieve in the flour and beat until the mixture forms a stiff dough.
• Place the dough on a sheet of baking paper and place another sheet on top. Gently press down with a rolling pin and roll out to 3–5 mm/⅛–¼ inch thick. Remove the top sheet of paper and stamp out circles from the dough using a 7-cm/2¾-inch round biscuit cutter. Re-knead and re-roll the trimmings and stamp out more biscuits.
• Using a palette knife, carefully transfer the biscuits to the prepared baking sheet. Prick them with a fork and bake in the preheated oven for 12 minutes, or until pale brown. Remove from the oven, cool on the baking sheet for 2 minutes, then transfer to a wire rack to cool completely.

Index